SHRIMP 'N LOBSTER

WRITTEN AND
ILLUSTRATED BY
CHARLOTTE RYGH

A NEW ENGLAND ADVENTURE

THE
collective
BOOK STUDIO

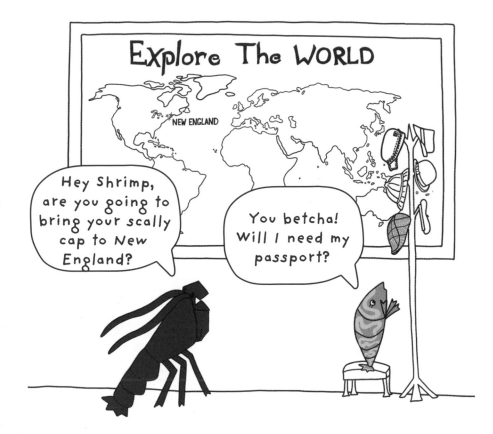

Design by David Miles

ISBN: 978-1-951412-35-7
LCCN: 2021902329

Manufactured in China

10 9 8 7 6 5 4 3 2 1

The Collective Book Studio®
Oakland, California
www.thecollectivebook.studio

CONTENTS

WELCOME, FELLOW EXPLORERS, TO YOUR PERSONAL GUIDE THROUGH NEW ENGLAND.

When you sign your name here, you are making a commitment to two rules for this tour:

1 Have fun!

2 Be kind and respectful to the people and nature around you.

THIS SHRIMP 'N LOBSTER EXPLORATION BOOK BELONGS TO:

Look! A quote from a fellow New England explorer!

"Here in New England, the character is strong and unshakable."

—Norman Rockwell, American Painter

As you explore any new place, you might feel a little bit out of your comfort zone. The best way to get comfortable? Ask questions!

WHAT TO PACK

New England has four full seasons with some serious weather in each. When Mr. Winter arrives, he sticks around for five months—from November through March. We're talkin' supercold, subarctic temperatures! Wear long underwear, scarves, hats, gloves, and a heavy coat to keep away that bone-chilling cold. We'll make a tough New Englander out of you in no time.

When spring arrives and flowers begin to bloom, chuck the heavy stuff. Some days are pretty warm and others might still be pretty cool, so a light jacket will do the trick.

Once summer hits, expect hot and humid. Pack light with T-shirts, tank tops, dresses, and shorts. Stay hydrated!

Temperatures will drop in the fall, so dig out your long sleeves and warm coats; it will get chilly at night. This is when the leaves turn from green to red, yellow, and orange— New England's trademark season. *Don't forget to pack your camera!*

NEW ENGLAND

Located in the northeast corner of the United States, New England consists of six states: Massachusetts, Maine, New Hampshire, Vermont, Connecticut, and Rhode Island. Each one of these states is super unique! Explore the seaside towns of Connecticut. Time travel to one of America's earliest colonies in Massachusetts. Pull in your first "catch" of lobster in Maine. Take scenic drives over the classic covered bridges of New Hampshire. Glide down the ski slopes in Vermont. And step inside America's castles of Rhode Island. From mountains to beaches and everything in between, your expedition will be fully packed!

HOW TO USE THIS BOOK

Read, learn, color, explore. Along with each of the interesting, fun, and exciting places to visit, we've included two sections: "Fascinating & True" and "Things to See & Do." We hope these will give you a deeper understanding of the history behind some of the people and places that make New England so special, making you the ultimate interactive participant in your new surroundings—a wicked-cool explorer!

THE MAP

Before beginning our journey, let's look at the map! We'll be exploring mountains, lakes, coastal beaches, and even islands. You'll experience a variety of accents and phrases, too!

To get ready, let's dive into some jargon you'll hear as you travel around. When in Maine, keep an ear out for ayuh (ay-YUH), as in "aye, aye, captain!" It means "yes!" Got it? Ayuh!

Next, you don't want to bang out (Boston's term for "move quickly") this trip too fast or you might pass up a swamp donkey (Maine's term for "moose") or a creemee (Vermont's term for "soft-serve ice cream"). And you really don't want to come off as a flatlander (an "out-of-towner" in Vermont). We know it's going to be one wicked-fun ("extremely fun") trip!

MASSACHUSETTS

Welcome to the sixth state of the Union and the birthplace of our American Revolution. With cities and seaside villages, Massachusetts has more than 300 years of history to explore. Let's dig in and see what makes the Bay State unique.

BOSTON

The capital of Massachusetts, Boston is host to many firsts: from the oldest public park, university, and subway, to the first marathon (in 1807). Our trip starts here, a town nicknamed after popular baked legumes. Beantown, we're comin' for ya!

This is the United States' oldest public park (opened in 1634). With paths that crisscross its 50 acres, it's easy to explore. And, if you listen closely, you may hear the ghosts of America's first colonists whispering in the air. Put on your walking shoes—welcome to the Common!

✓ Originally, the Common was a cow pasture! A group of colonists purchased the land from Anglican minister William Blackstone in 1634, and called it common land. Looks like that phrase stuck and the cows moooved to the city.

. . . .

✓ When America was occupied by the British in 1775, the Common was a training field for more than 1,000 British soldiers, called Redcoats. This was the starting point for their march to Lexington and Concord and the battle that ignited the American Revolution.

. . . .

✓ The very first football game was played in the Common in 1862. *Hut, hut, hike!*

Shrimp 'n Lobster pond has a better ring to it, don't ya think?

Look! The carousel! A craftsmen masterpiece.

Visit Frog Pond any time of year. Splash around in the spray pool to cool off during the summer and carve some ice when it transforms into a winter skating rink. We only have ice for you!

Check out Parkman Bandstand. It has been the home of thousands of concerts and rallies that featured high-profile speakers such as Martin Luther King Jr., Charles Lindbergh, and President Barack Obama.

Look for the Robert Gould Shaw and the 54th Regiment Memorial. The bronze sculpture was dedicated in 1897. At just twenty-five years old, Colonel Shaw led the first volunteer Black regiment of the Civil War.

The Common is also the starting place of the Freedom Trail. This redbrick path around downtown is 2.5 miles long, so plan on a full day. You'll be visiting many sites that are important to the founding of our country.

What separates Boston Common from the Boston Public Garden? Charles Street and a mere 200-year age gap! Here you can cross a miniature bridge, ride in swan boats, and hang with bronze ducklings on the go. But let's not forget those superfancy flower beds.

FASCINATING & TRUE

✓ The Public Garden was established in 1837. It became the first botanical garden in the U.S. Years later, in 1859, architect George Meacham won a design contest to construct the twenty-four-acre Victorian-era garden, adding many of the attractions we see today.

✓ Mallard Island used to be a small peninsula that attracted a lot of lovebirds. But in 1880, the city tried to put a stop to that and cut the peninsula off, creating the serene island for some real "fowl play." Quack! Quack!

✓ The four-acre lake is manmade and only three-to-four feet deep. Although it's not an official skating rink, it's not uncommon to find someone gliding along in winter when the shallow water turns to ice.

THINGS TO SEE & DO

Explore the public art. Waddle over and take a selfie with Nancy Schön's *Make Way for Ducklings* sculpture installed in 1987 as a tribute to Robert McCloskey's beloved picture book by the same name. You might just find them dressed for the occasion!

Take a swan boat ride on the lagoon. As you cruise around Mallard Island, if you're lucky, in the spring you'll see ducklings swimming around their namesake.

See the Public Garden in full bloom! In early May, 25,000 tulips awaken from their winter slumber, creating a Technicolor wonder! It's nothing to sneeze at! And it may just take your breath away.

The Public Garden, along with Boston Common, belongs to a string of parks known as the "Emerald Necklace." This 1,100-acre chain of parks is linked by parkways and waterways in Boston and neighboring Brookline.

GRANARY BURYING GROUND

TREMONT STREET

This is the final resting spot for some serious American Revolutionary heroes and founding fathers, including John Hancock and Paul Revere. As you walk around, take care because some of these tombstones are older than our country—more than 350 years and counting!

FASCINATING & TRUE

✓ The Granary was created in 1660 but didn't get its official name until 1737. It's named after the neighboring grain storage building called Old Town Granary. Bread, anyone?

....

✓ In 1770, a street fight between some colonists and a British soldier grew into what's now known as the Boston Massacre. Five of its victims are resting here. This brawl energized the colonists to secede from England and paved the way for the Revolutionary War.

....

✓ The headstones are only the tip of the iceberg. While there are roughly 2,300 tombstones in the cemetery, people believe that up to 5,000 bodies are buried here. It was more affordable and space-conscious to bury the dead one on top of the other.

See if you can find three signers of the Declaration of Independence: Samuel Adams, John Hancock, and Robert Treat Paine.

. . . .

Find the obelisk. It stands twenty-five feet tall and celebrates the parents of Benjamin Franklin. You can't miss it! (Although Ben was a huge Bostonian, he is buried at Christ Church Burial Ground in Philadelphia.)

. . . .

Look for elaborately carved tombstones with figures like the Grim Reaper, Father Time, and a skull in flight with two wings. These are the oldest symbols of death found throughout New England, dating from 1640 to the late 18th century.

. . . .

FRANKLIN

The obelisk is a fascinating choice for a tombstone...

Maybe that's the point! Ha-ha-ha!

SAMVEL GRAY
SAMVEL MAVERICK
JAMES CALDWELL
CRISPVS ATTVCKS

PATRICK CARR

Victims of the Boston Massacre
March 5th, 1770.
were here interred by order of the
Town of Boston.

Here also lies buried the body of
CHRISTOPHER SNIDER

Aged 12 years
Killed February 22nd 1770
The innocent, first victim of the
struggles between the Colonists and
the Crown, which resulted in
INDEPENDENCE

Placed by Boston Chapter S.A.R.
1906

W NEAL
8 MONTHS

23

Enhance your creativity and imagination as you explore this interactive space, first funded by public school teachers more than 100 years ago! The museum teaches visitors that life's real lessons go beyond the textbook, making it feel like a superfun playground. Let's check it out!

Just because you're a shrimp doesn't mean you're small. Let's go!

FASCINATING & TRUE

✓ The Boston Children's Museum was ahead of its time when it first opened in 1913. Its goal is hands-on learning and observation, including taking nature hikes. *Now that's something we'd sign up for!*

....

✓ The Boston museum has a collection of more than 50,000 items to explore! From science, visual arts, performing arts, and natural history to Japanese artifacts and much, much more!

....

✓ In 1979, the city of Kyoto, Japan, gifted the museum a 100-year-old house of a Japanese silk merchant. Explore this beautiful home, but remember their custom: Take your shoes off before you enter, please. *Domo arigato!*

....

THINGS TO SEE & DO

For the love of bubbles, this is one stop that will have you deep in the suds! Experiment with a variety of tools to make the perfect soapy floater; large or small, you'll be a bubble master in no time!

....

Come face-to-face with a life-sized dinosaur that visitors can touch and manipulate! You can find the sharp-toothed carnivore Dilophosaurus at the Explore-a-Saurus exhibit. Perhaps you'll even dig up some interesting conclusions as you observe its fossilized footprints.

....

If you like mazes, then you'll love the three-story New Balance Foundation Climb. The only way to find the best path is to try it out for yourself. It's a-maze-ing!

Woohoo! This is one net I don't mind getting stuck in.

Don't get caught up in that for too long!

This seaside aquarium is home to 20,000 animals from all around the globe. Visit creatures from the deep sea, tropical rainforests, mangroves, and coral reefs. Dive in, but leave your snorkel behind as you'll be exploring without getting wet.

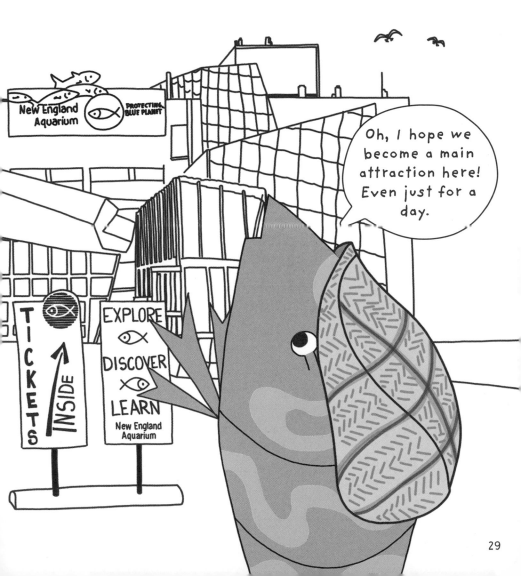

FASCINATING & TRUE

✓ The Giant Ocean Tank, a central feature of the aquarium, is a Caribbean coral reef exhibit that is forty feet wide and four stories tall. It's filled with 200,000 gallons of seawater and is home to more than 1,000 tropical fish. When can we move in?

. . . .

✓ The mangrove-themed shark and ray touch-tank is the largest on the east coast. With 25,000 gallons, it allows you to come face to face with a more gentle side of the aquarium.

. . . .

✓ Did you know the African penguin sounds like a jackass . . . we mean donkey? That's also their nickname: jackass penguins. Listen for yourself at the Penguin Colony Exhibit. Additionally, the water from the penguin colony is taken from Boston Harbor!

. . . .

THINGS TO SEE & DO

Say hello to Myrtle, a green sea turtle and the Aquarium's mascot. She's lived here since 1970! You can visit this 500-pound swimmer in the Giant Ocean Tank. If you're lucky, maybe she'll take a selfie with you!

. . . .

The Amazon Rainforest exhibit is a must-see that brings you face to face with flesh-eating piranhas, bone-crushing anacondas, vibrant dart frogs, and shocking electric eels!

. . . .

In both indoor and outdoor exhibits, visit our favorite pinnipeds—that means mammals with all four limbs modified into flippers. The harbor seals and northern fur seals will amaze you with their grace and skills.

. . . .

FANEUIL HALL

4 SOUTH MARKET STREET

When Faneuil Hall was completed in 1742, it became the go-to place for bigwigs *(those are important people, Lobster)* and superpatriots as they pushed for independence from England. It wasn't just the food that brought the locals to this marketplace: the hot topic was always how to make King George III their ex-landlord. These discussions led to some people calling Faneuil Hall "the Cradle of Liberty."

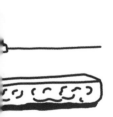

FASCINATING & TRUE

✓ Peter Faneuil, who made his wealth through selling goods such as molasses, fish, wine, timber, and even African slaves *(Shame on him!)*, recognized the need for a central marketplace in the booming town.

. . . .

✓ The famed hall became a pre–Revolutionary War meeting place. But when it became so overstuffed with politicians, colonial leaders, and Bostonians, they had to move to the Old South Meeting House, a historic church that is known as an organizing place for the Boston Tea Party.

. . . .

✓ After a third story was added in the 19th century, the market continued to expand, including North Market, Quincy Market, and South Market, and hosting both indoor and outdoor shopping starting in the 1970s.

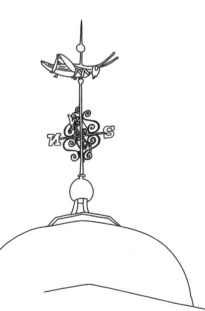

. . . .

THINGS TO SEE & DO

Summertime at Faneuil Hall features amazing street performers in the open square. Historical reenactments, magicians, dancers, comics, and musicians—it's all here. If you want to get serious, watch the Street Performers Festival on Memorial Day Weekend. It attracts performers from around the world to strut their stuff. Auditions only. Do you have the acting chops?

....

Go crazy and explore the local merchants and their shops—now more than forty of them—just as the locals did three hundred years ago.

....

See if you can spot the Golden Grasshopper weathervane. He's been there since he hopped up in 1742!

....

This is another stop on the Freedom Trail!

....

PAUL REVERE HOUSE

19 NORTH SQUARE

*L*earn what it was like to live during the 18th century in the home of superpatriot Paul Revere. Located in the North End section of Boston (today it's called Little Italy), the neighborhood attracted artisans, merchants, and tradesmen. For Paul, who was a silversmith, the location couldn't be more fitting.

FASCINATING & TRUE

✓ Hey, guess what? You're standing in the oldest building in town! This three-story dwelling was built around 1680, more than three centuries ago. Now that's a strong foundation!

✓ In April 18, 1775, Paul Revere took off from this spot with his steady steed and two friends, William Dawes and Samuel Prescott. The famed "midnight ride" warned Samuel Adams and John Hancock in nearby Lexington that "the British are coming!"

✓ When you're on the Freedom Trail, this is one stop you won't want to miss.

Check out the Paul Revere Mall. There you'll find thirteen tablets that honor famous former residents of Boston. Look for John Hull on Plaque 4. He created the first U.S. Mint and the first American money. The creation of the coin represented independence from England. That's no chump change!

Visit the famous statue of Paul Revere designed by sculptor Cyrus E. Dallin. You can find it in front of the Old North Church. It's one of the top photo ops in town, so be sure to take a few snaps for yourself.

OLD NORTH CHURCH

193 SALEM STREET

The lobsterboats are coming! The lobsterboats are coming! Ha! Ha! Ha! Get it?

Dwarfed by modern skyscrapers, you wouldn't have guessed that when this church opened in 1723, it was the tallest building in town. It also became famous for being the logical place for the "one if by land, two if by sea" signal that warned that the British troops were about to attack.

FASCINATING & TRUE

✓ The Old North Church was Anglican—that means it was a church of England! Those who attended were considered to be loyal to the British. Imagine how those Brits felt when they learned that the Old North was used as a beacon for independence?

· ·

✓ A custodian of the church, Robert Newman, and church member John Pulling climbed up the 154 winding steps to the bell tower to quietly display two lanterns, a signal that the British troops were on their way—by sea.

· ·

✓ The steeple at Old North Church was originally funded by ship captain Newark Jackson, a merchant and chocolatier. Don't let his business fool you into thinking he was a sweetie; he was involved in the Caribbean slave trade.

· ·

DRAW THE CANDLES USED IN THOSE LANTERNS AND LIGHT THE WAY TO ALERT THE AMERICAN PATRIOTS.

THINGS TO SEE & DO

Look for the bust of George Washington! According to French superpatriot Marquis de Lafayette, the carving is the spitting image of the first president of the United States. Magnifique!

....

Learn how to make chocolate as they did in the 18th century at the Historic Chocolate Program. Reenactors will not only show you how pre—Revolution-era people made this sweet treat, but also tell you how it became a booming business for merchants and traders.

....

Amazingly, you can still see one of the two famous lanterns from the Old North Church that led to the American Revolution.

....

You're on a roll! This is all still on the Freedom Trail!

....

What was it again? One if by sea or two if by land? I forget. Fortunately, Mr. Revere and his friends got it right!

USS CONSTITUTION
BUILDING 22, CHARLESTOWN NAVY YARD

The USS Constitution is docked at the port where she was originally built, right in the Charlestown Navy Yard that is currently a part of the Boston National Historical Park. Nicknamed "Old Ironsides" for the way enemy cannonballs bounced off her flanks, she continues to proudly serve as the Navy's oldest commissioned vessel.

Look! The oldest military ship in the country!

FASCINATING & TRUE

✓ President George Washington named the proudly Charlestown—born ship the USS *Constitution*. Inspiration came from . . . well, we bet you can guess which historic document.

....

✓ This mega-warship was launched in 1797. She was one of the six original frigates of the U.S. Navy. Their designs were much larger and fortified than earlier warships, making them superscary to any would-be invaders.

....

✓ The *Constitution* was built in the North End of Boston—that's also where our superpatriot Paul Revere lived. He supplied the copper and brass fittings for the ship, not to mention the 242-pound bell! Ding ding!

....

✓ The charming "Old Ironsides" nickname was a real lifesaver— her fame kept her from the scrapyard.

....

THINGS TO SEE & DO

☐ Explore this historic vessel and imagine yourself as one of more than 450 sailors in her crew. Navy crew members will be there to assist you. Make their day fun, too—ask about the difference between the poop deck and the head.

....

☐ Learn about the war that made the USS Constitution famous when you visit the "Old Ironsides" War of 1812 Discovery Center in the USS Constitution Museum.

....

☐ Take part in "All Hands on Deck" to explore a day in the life of a sailor. Scrub that deck, eat those salted meats, learn how to tie a proper sailor's knot, all while avoiding scurvy . . . most important, listen to the officers' first-hand accounts of their battles during the War of 1812.

....

☐ You're near the end of the Freedom Trail!

....

BUNKER HILL MONUMENT

MONUMENT SQUARE

Bunker Hill Monument is one of the first monuments erected in the United States. It commemorates the first major battle between patriot and British soldiers on June 17, 1775, during the British siege of Boston.

FASCINATING & TRUE

✓ Bunker Hill Monument took more than seventeen years to build; it was completed in 1843. With 6,700 tons of local granite rising 221 feet, it became the nation's tallest memorial. That is until the famed Washington Monument in Washington, D.C., took the title in 1888.

✓ The hill on which the monument stands is actually named Breed's Hill, which is where most of the fighting took place. Breed's Hill is next to Bunker Hill—both were important because whoever gained control of the hills would then control Boston Harbor. The battle was mistakenly called Bunker Hill, and, well, the rest is history.

✓ The statue of war hero William Prescott was erected in 1881. He was famously quoted as telling his young troops, "Do not fire until you see the whites of their eyes."

◻ While inside Bunker Hill lodge, visit the statue of the fallen hero Dr. Joseph Warren, who lost his life in the Battle of Bunker Hill. He is responsible for enlisting Paul Revere and his companions, William Dawes and Samuel Prescott, to spread the word on April 18, 1775, that the British were coming.

....

◻ Climb to the memorial's observation deck. Don't expect any shortcuts because, with no elevator, you've got 294 spiraling stairs to conquer. You've got this! The reward is an epic view of Boston and Charlestown.

....

◻ You're at the last stop on the Freedom Trail!

....

THE T

When you're not walking, the next best thing is to jump on the T! This fast and supereasy mode of public transportation can take you around the city in no time. And who cares if there's a delay? You're in Boston. Enjoy the sights!

FASCINATING & TRUE

✓ The Massachusetts Bay Transportation Authority, also known as the MBTA or just the T, gets you where you need to go. It manages the subway, bus, train, and ferry services as well as the RIDE service that helps those with disabilities.

....

✓ Boston is home to the very first subway tunnels in North America! The Green Line made its official debut on September 2, 1897, making it 124 years old and climbing.

....

✓ You have five color-designated lines from which to choose for a supereasy commute: Orange, Blue, Green, Red, and Silver. The Blue Line, built in 1904, will even take you under the Charles River! We'd rather swim, but you probably want to stay dry.

....

If you're eleven years old or younger, you get to ride free with one paying adult. Now there's no reason you can't go out and explore this city! As for everyone else, keep your ticket. You'll need it to take advantage of any free transfers.

Enjoy the Green Line, which operates as a street trolley aboveground as well as an underground subway. Additionally, it will take you through most of the Emerald Necklace, which is how the line got its name! Be sure you jump off to visit all nine wonderful public parks.

If you explore the Red Line, exit at Harvard Square and explore Harvard University. The Red Line also got its name from Harvard's school color—crimson!

BACK BAY

Explore this fancy neighborhood that is famous for its 19th-century architecture. It's a popular gathering spot with hotels, museums, libraries, and galleries. Oh yeah, it also happens to be the home of the tallest building in town.

FASCINATING & TRUE

✓ The Boston Public Library, located at Copley Square, opened in 1848. With 600,000 books, it grew to become the largest free public library in the world. Today it stands second, next to the Library of Congress. No wonder it was called "a palace for the people."

✓ The John Hancock Tower, also called "The Hancock," rises sixty-two stories, making it the tallest building in New England!

HOWS MY DRIVING?

The Prudential building, dead ahead!

Investigate the murals at Trinity Church, which was founded in 1733. The paintings cover 21,500 square feet of wall space. Painter John La Farge wanted to inspire "the feeling that you are walking into a painting."

Step inside a three-story-tall stained-glass globe at the Mapparium. Located in the Mary Baker Eddy Library, the globe offers an enormous inside-out view of the world. Chart out your next destination!

Look up and check the next day's weather at the illuminated beacon at the top of the Berkeley Building, built in 1947. The beacon's red and blue lights indicate the weather forecast (blue means clear skies ahead; red means rain is coming).

Rest your feet and let a duck boat do the touring for you. The ninety-minute rides will take you around the town—and into the Charles River—in World War II—era amphibious landing vehicles. FULL STEAM AHEAD!

Can we park in front so we don't have to walk?

FENWAY PARK

4 JERSEY STREET

THINGS TO SEE & DO

Welcome to Fenway Park, the home of the Boston Red Sox baseball team. Located in the heart of downtown Boston, it's one of the nation's most beloved stadiums—and oldest! Whether you walk, ride a bike, or take public transportation, getting there is easy for you to enjoy this all-American game with some diehard fans. *Play ball!*

- Visit statues of baseball legends at Gate B: Ted Williams, Bobby Doerr, Johnny Pesky, and Dom DiMaggio (one of three baseball playing DiMaggio brothers).

- Eat your way through the game. Try the slammin' onions, s'mores, bread pudding, lobster BLTs, and Yankee lobster rolls. Sheesh! The food has come a long way since the classic hot dog.

- Look for a bright red seat! This spot in the right field bleachers is where Red Sox legend Ted Williams hit a monster 502-foot home run back on June 9, 1946.

✓ The ballpark was constructed in just one year, and the first official game was played on April 20, 1912, against the archrival New York Highlanders (now called the Yankees).

....

✓ In 1915, a young Red Sox pitcher named Babe Ruth hit his very first home run out of the park. Years later, in a trade that many Boston fans still argue over, Ruth was traded to the Yankees, where he made history. And Boston had to wait eighty-six years to win a championship! Ahhh, *the Curse of the Bambino!*

....

✓ There's a green monster at the ballpark . . . well, sort of. When the ballpark was built, owner John Taylor asked for a 25-foot wall to prevent fans outside the park from viewing the games for free. When it was painted green in the 1940s, the deal was sealed: the "Green Monster" was born.

....

TEAMMATES

Seven miles from downtown Boston, located on Georges Island at the entrance to Boston Harbor, stands the Fort Warren military compound and defense post. It was designed to protect the city from would-be invaders. Today, it's a National Historic Landmark and leaves its doors open to explorers like us!

FASCINATING & TRUE

✓ Fort Warren was completed just as the Civil War broke out in 1861, after twenty years of construction.

....

✓ The fort's classic five-sided shape includes five bastions, or arrowhead-like corners, that protect the fort from all sides. Oh yeah, there's a moat, too.

....

✓ This was also a training ground for Union soldiers and a prison for Confederate officers and government officials. The most famous inmate was Alexander Hamilton, the vice president of the Confederate States (the Confederacy broke away from the U.S., causing the Civil War).

....

✓ You might have already guessed it, but Fort Warren was named after the Revolutionary hero Joseph Warren. You met his famous statue at the Bunker Hill Lodge!

....

THINGS TO SEE & DO

Enjoy the 45-minute boat ride to the island!
While you're out there, take in the scenery. This
is sea-faring country—you'll face the wind as our
forefathers once did.

Take a guided tour of the island and investigate
the Lady in Black. Legend has it that her ghost still
haunts the grounds. Ask the park rangers about
her story and where she's recently been seen. Be
warned, you might need to keep the light on to help
you sleep at night.

Fort Warren is a five-sided fort. Can you name
another famous pentagonal-shaped building? The
clue is in the question!

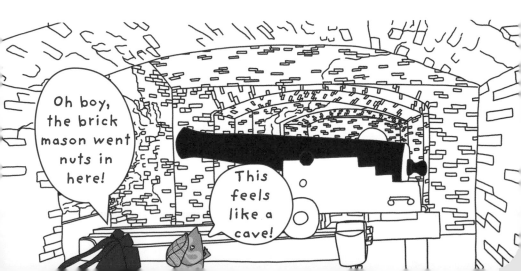

SALEM

You don't have to wait for Halloween to stir up some witches' brew. This tiny historical town invites everyone to explore its streets, museums, shops, and cemeteries. See if you can find out the truth behind what ignited the most haunting trials in the early 17th century, the Salem Witch Trials.

✓ The Salem Witch Trials took place between February 1692 and May 1693. More than 200 people were convicted of practicing witchcraft, aka "the devil's magic." Further, nineteen people were hung, one was pressed to death, and many others were imprisoned.

....

✓ The Witch House is the residence of superwealthy Jonathan Corwin, one of the judges who sentenced nineteen people to their deaths. It's the last standing structure connected to the trials.

....

✓ Halloween attracts 250,000 visiting witches and warlocks every year. Come have some spooky fun *witch* us!

....

THINGS TO SEE & DO

Follow the Salem Heritage Trail. Marked by a red line on the sidewalk, it will take you to all the historic sites in town!

. . . .

Visit the Salem Witch Museum. Learn what life was like in 17th-century Salem and what brought on the witch hunts.

. . . .

Tour the Witch House, Judge Jonathan Corwin's home! See how Puritans lived during the late 1600s.

. . . .

Step into Ye Ole Pepper Company, America's oldest candy maker! Taste their original Salem Gibraltars and Black Jacks. Look for the jar of 173-year-old Gibraltars! We're guessing they're as hard as a (Plymouth) rock!

. . . .

In the winter of 1620, a ship called the Mayflower arrived at Plymouth and started the American journey. Only half of the original 102 Pilgrims survived the harsh weather their first year. A granite rock became the symbol of their unwavering determination. And an annual American feast found its roots. And we're not talkin' potatoes and carrots!

I've got a butter idea, let's check out the Mayflower II!

FASCINATING & TRUE

✓ Before the *Mayflower* returned to England, the Pilgrims lived aboard the ship as they built their homes from scratch! Moving-in day was March 1621.

. . . .

✓ The colonists celebrated surviving their first year, and first fall harvest, with a three-day festival with the Wampanoag Native Americans. Today we call it Thanksgiving.

. . . .

✓ Plymouth Rock was pointed out (literally) 121 years later by 94-year-old Thomas Faunce as the very spot that the colonists (his father included) first stepped onto land. But wait! They actually all disembarked in Provincetown on Cape Cod first. This tall tale sounds a little fishy to us!

. . . .

✓ The rock has been dropped, chiseled, and cracked until making its home in a Roman-like temple in 1920. There's even a chunk at the Smithsonian in Washington, D.C.

☐ Visit Plymouth Rock, the landing place of the Pilgrims. This ten-ton granite rock is surrounded by a giant-columned memorial. You can't miss it!

· ·

☐ Find the statue of the late governor and English Puritan William Bradford. He later wrote a book about his experience called *Of Plymouth Plantation*. Check it out!

· ·

☐ Look for the statue of Massasoit Sachem, leader of the Wampanoags. He secured the first peace treaty in 1621 between the Native Americans and the colonists.

· ·

☐ Time travel to the 17th century and see how the Pilgrims and the Wampanoag Native Americans lived at the Plimoth Plantation. (That's the original spelling!)

· ·

☐ Visit Burial Hill cemetery, one of Plymouth's oldest cemeteries and the resting spot for more than 2,500 people, including the famed William Bradford.

· ·

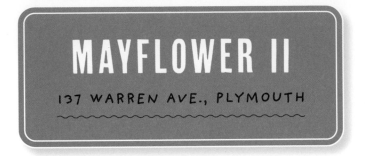

MAYFLOWER II

137 WARREN AVE., PLYMOUTH

The *Mayflower II* is a replica of the original ship that set sail from England for a 66-day journey to the Americas in 1620. You can visit this vessel and learn how the Pilgrims survived the dangerous voyage and made Plymouth their new home. She also made the U.S. National Register of Historic Places.

FASCINATING & TRUE

✓ The recently restored *Mayflower II* was handcrafted in England using blueprints from the American museum and 17th-century building techniques.

. . . .

✓ This American treasure was designed to celebrate the relationship between England and the United States during WWII. What a sea-worthy tribute!

. . . .

✓ The original *Mayflower* was designed as a merchant ship to transport goods, meaning the passengers' sleeping and living quarters were the superdark cargo hold.

. . . .

✓ When the *Mayflower* returned to England on April 5, 1621, she was most likely sold for scrap. Yowch!

. . . .

THINGS TO SEE & DO

Board this historic vessel and learn about what it was like to sail on 17th-century merchant ships.

· ·

You don't have to be the captain—we mean the master—on this vessel to check out his living space. Enter the private domain of Captain Christopher Jones. It's definitely more comfortable than what the passengers and crew were given. It's nice to be the big honcho!

· ·

We love asking questions! Find a friendly reenactor—you can't miss them dressed in 17th-century clothes. They can tell you all about this amazing ship and the history that built our first settlement.

· ·

That's it? But it's so small.

The Mayflower survived two months at sea and still had to face a New England winter.

CAPE COD

This historic seaside destination is most popular in the summer, especially for its beaches, supercute villages, and seafood! Explore more than 500 miles of coastline in the shape of an elf's shoe, and see why the Cape is one of the top New England destinations to visit.

FASCINATING & TRUE

✓ First Encounter Beach in Eastham is the spot where the Pilgrims and Native Americans first met in 1620. You can guess how the beach got its name—there's a plaque commemorating the event.

. . . .

✓ Pilgrim Monument in Provincetown ("P-town" to the locals!) is designed after a tower located in Siena, Italy, called the Torre del Mangia. It's also the tallest all-granite structure in the country, standing at 252 feet! Magnifico! Andiamo!

. . . .

✓ Cape Cod is home to fourteen historical lighthouses, the most famous and photographed being the Nauset Light. They'll light your world.

. . . .

Explore the Pilgrim Monument and Provincetown Museum. Learn more about the Wampanoag Native Americans and the Mayflower Pilgrims.

. . . .

Visit Woods Hole Oceanographic Institution, WHOI ("who-ee") for short! You won't need sonar to find the *Titanic* here. Learn how WHOI scientist Robert Ballard found the ill-fated ship in the *Titanic* exhibit. Step inside Alvin, the deep-diving submersible, or tune in to the song of whales . . . and that's just the tip of the iceberg.

. . . .

Dine at the Lobster Pot in P-town, where they've been serving a New England staple . . . um, lobster, since 1943. *We'll skip that one, if you don't mind.*

. . . .

Take a bike ride! The Cape Cod Rail Trail and the Shining Sea Bike Path are both paved so that you can safely explore the Cape on two wheels instead of four.

. . . .

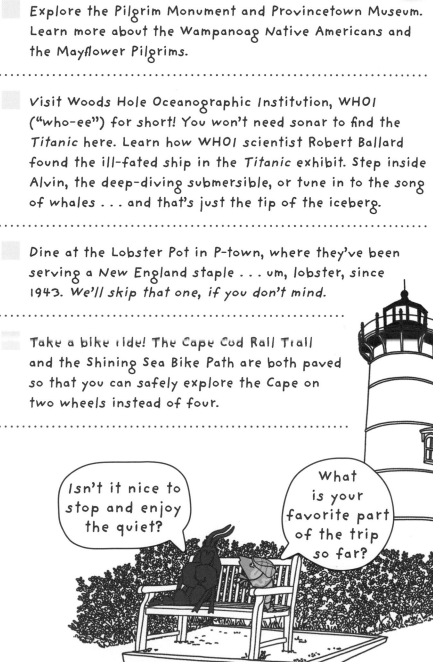

Isn't it nice to stop and enjoy the quiet?

What is your favorite part of the trip so far?

MAINE

Usually when you think of Maine, one thing comes to mind: lobster! But it's also famous for Acadia National Park, moose, and the original Whoopie Pie. They even host a festival for their famous sweet treat. Let's dive in and see what this state is all about . . . avoiding all the lobster traps, of course.

Look! The first light to hit the United States.

ACADIA NATIONAL PARK

Enjoy a visit to Mount Desert Island, one of the smallest national parks in the country! Join the more than 3.5 million guests who walk, bike, take the bus, and even ride a horse on these majestic 49,000 acres every year. Don't forget to pose at Rockefeller's Teeth while you're there. Say, "Big cheese!"

FASCINATING & TRUE

✓ Acadia was established on July 8, 1916, by Woodrow Wilson as the first National Park in the North Atlantic.

✓ Cadillac Mountain is the tallest mountain on the Atlantic coast, rising 1,530 feet high. It is also the first point in the U.S. to see sunlight between October and early March.

✓ There are 45 miles of carriage roads. They were a gift from our favorite New York moneyman, John D. Rockefeller Jr., who loved exploring this park on horseback. No loud cars on this expedition . . . just peace and quiet.

THINGS TO SEE & DO

☐ Jump on the free Island Explorer Bus. It will take you to trailheads, carriage roads, beaches, shops, and restaurants, making it supereasy to explore!

....

☐ Hike up Cadillac Mountain. It can take between 2.5 to 4 hours to reach the top. If you time it correctly, you may just see the first sunup.

....

☐ Explore the carriage roads as John D. Rockefeller Jr. did and look for Rockefeller's Teeth! They are the large granite stones that line the roads.

....

PORTLAND

This southern seaside community is home to two-thirds of Maine's residents. What makes this such a popular spot? The food, history, and beauty, not to mention ALL that lobster! We'll take the compliment . . . without the melted butter and garlic.

✓ In the early 1600s, Portland, originally called Falmouth, was the northernmost destination for early English settlers.

✓ The Portland Head Light is the oldest lighthouse in Maine. It's also the most photographed in America! Its location has a long history of protecting the locals. Prior to the lighthouse being built, eight soldiers would stand guard at that point to look out for British ships.

✓ Local legend says the Calendar Islands in Casco Bay got their name because each island represented one day in the year. Looks like their math was wrong: there are actually 785 not 365!

THINGS TO SEE & DO

☐ Explore the Harbor Fish Market in Old Port. You'll quickly SEA . . . we mean, SEE, what treasures the North Atlantic provides.

. . . .

☐ Take part in a Maine lobster tour and learn all about our favorite crustacean! And how to sustainably catch us . . . uh . . . THEM. It might be the Maine attraction of your trip!

. . . .

☐ Rent a kayak and tour the calm waters of Casco Bay. You've got hundreds of islands to explore . . . take them in and enjoy the ocean just as we do.

. . . .

☐ Visit the super-old Portland Head Light! At the former keeper's house, you'll learn how these lighthouses safely lit the way for sailors.

. . . .

☐ Check out the mysterious International Cryptozoology Museum, where the quirky exhibits range from hair of the Abominable Snowman to a plaster cast of Bigfoot's footprint. Do these beings exist? You be the judge.

. . . .

Welcome to *New Hampshire*—the Granite State, the White Mountain State, the Switzerland of America. It's famous for the highest peak in New England, fifty-four covered bridges, and a world-renowned bodega. It was also the first colony to vote for independence from Britain, creating the motto "Live Free or Die." Talk about one trailblazing state!

This is the life!

SACO RIVER FLOAT

WHITE MOUNTAINS

The White Mountains are located in the White Mountain National Forest, covering one-quarter of the state! From nail-biting train rides to relaxing river floats and picturesque carriage bridges, the White Mountains will certainly awaken the outdoor enthusiast within you.

✓ Mount Washington is the tallest peak in New England, reaching 6,288 feet high, and holds the title for "world's worst weather," making it the perfect training ground for mountain climbers before they hit the big leagues like Everest and K2. In 1934, the peak's observatory recorded the world's strongest wind gust at 231 miles per hour!

....

✓ There has been a resident cat at the observatory since 1932! Purrrrfect company for lodging scientists, and not so good for others. SQUEAK! SQUEAK!

....

✓ New Hampshire is famous for its covered bridges. The oldest is the Bath-Haverhill Covered Bridge, built in 1829. Why are the bridges covered? To protect the structures from all that bad weather.

....

Can I sit in the front now?

WAUMBEK

☐ Take the Cog Railway up to the Mount Washington Observatory. This powerful train is designed to handle superhilly climbs. It's is the second-steepest ascent in the world (the steepest is in Switzerland), and has thrilled visitors since 1869.

☐ Visit Zeb's General Store in North Conway. This store is a great spot for maple . . . anything! Even if you don't have a sweet tooth, you'll find something yummy. More than 80 percent of their goods are home crafted in New England. We LOVE supporting local businesses!

☐ Grab an inner tube and head to the clear waters of the Saco River. Float or paddle your way down the river, and take a spin on a rope swing. You'll have a splashing good time!

79

PORTSMOUTH

This seaside town at the mouth of the Piscataqua River was founded in 1623, making it New Hampshire's oldest settlement. Early merchants were able to do some serious trading here, making it one of New England's most thriving seaports and shipyards.

THINGS TO SEE & DO

Look for the 150-foot-tall white steeple of the North Church, built in 1657. It's a great landmark to help you know where you are in the town.

Explore the 17th-century historic homes of Strawberry Banke Museum. This ten-acre, open-air museum is the oldest neighborhood in New Hampshire to be settled by Europeans.

Cruise the bay and check out the historic skyline. Keep an eye out for the maroon and black Moran Tugboats. You can't miss the giant "M" on the side; they've been tugging and towing vessels since 1860.

✓ In 1630, colonists named their new settlement Strawberry Banke due to the abundance of wild strawberries growing in the area. It was renamed Portsmouth in 1653.

....

✓ This bustling 17th-century seaport relied on agriculture, fishing, shipbuilding, and timber. Its darker past included slave trade. Many goods were exported to England. Remember, prior to the Revolutionary War, what they produced went straight to the Crown. It was good to be King!

....

✓ This still-working port includes the first Federal Navy Shipyard, established in 1800. Call it a "ship hospital" for cruisers that need upgrades. This shipyard also built the first submarine!

....

Wahoo! The open sea!

We're just cruising the Bay!

PORTSMOUTH HARBOR CRUISES

HERITAGE

LAKE WINNIPESAUKEE

Lake Winnipesaukee, also called "Lake Winnie" by locals, has attracted vacationers since before the Revolutionary War. It was basically the first colonial resort town. With watersports, beachside towns, and wildlife, you will quickly understand why this lake continues to attract visitors as it did more than 250 years ago.

FASCINATING & TRUE

✓ You're visiting the largest lake in New Hampshire. It stretches 28 miles long and 9.5 miles wide, including 365 islands for you to explore—one for every day of the year. (Sound familiar?)

✓ Offering shops, restaurants, and water activities, the town of Wolfeboro is the oldest summer resort in America—a "club" where vacationers have been coming since 1770.

✓ The *Sophie C* is the oldest floating post office in the U.S. She has been delivering mail to island residents since 1892. Additionally, *Sophie* is a tour boat, combining both work and pleasure!

THINGS TO SEE & DO

Cruise on the MS *Mount Washington*. This passenger boat has been touring Winnie for 148 years and counting!

....

Check out the Squam Lakes Natural Science Center in Holderness. Their 200-acre campus offers educational programs, lake tours, and live-animal exhibits.

....

Enjoy a two-hour old-fashioned train ride along the shore on the Hobo & Winnipesaukee Scenic Railroad. CHOO-CHOO!

....

Write a postcard about your Winnie adventure! Make it official with a *Sophie C* postmark. She'll ship it out for ya, too!

....

VERMONT

With mountains, lakes, and ice cream, the Green Mountain state is a haven for nature lovers and outdoor enthusiasts. Vermont has a deep revolutionary past and provided strong support for the Underground Railroad. You'll be singing, skiing, hiking, and scooping out the sweet life in Vermont.

LAKE CHAMPLAIN

Welcome to the lake that crosses the boundaries of two states and two countries. From Vermont and New York to Quebec, Canada, Champlain covers 490 square miles. It has been called "the waterway to freedom," and "the blue highway" for being a "line" on the Underground Railroad. Oh yeah, there's a little monster living there called Champy, too.

I hope this works!

Maybe our lake monster will go viral!

FASCINATING & TRUE

✓ The waterways that leave this lake reach all the way to Manhattan, 300 miles away! You can also cruise to Canada. Don't forget your passport!

✓ The lake is a permanent home to roughly 300 shipwrecks, some as deep as 100 feet. The oldest dates back to the Revolutionary War. Bring your scuba tank to take a deep dive into history.

✓ In the 1800s, many slaves escaped across this body of water to seek freedom and a better life. Their journey can be seen at the North Star Underground Railroad Museum (take a ferry over to New York).

THINGS TO SEE & DO

- Take a seven-minute ride on the Fort Ticonderoga Ferry, the oldest ferry crossing in North America! Beginning in 1759, it carried British troops from Lake Champlain to the Connecticut River during the French and Indian War.

- Visit the Lake Champlain Maritime Museum. Learn how to build and maintain wooden boats, take part in a youth rowing team, or explore shipwrecks! You may just want a captain's hat after this expedition.

- If you enjoy fishing (*GULP!*), grab a pole, because you're in bass country. Lake Champlain is considered one of the top places to fish for bass in the whole country.

- Look up! The lake is a migratory path for many birds, including snow geese. These birds travel more than 3,000 miles to and from the Arctic in the spring and fall.

TRAPP FAMILY LODGE

700 TRAPP HILL ROAD, STOWE

Time to practice your yodel! Because a tiny slice of Austria is nestled in the hills of Vermont— all brought to you by the supermusical von Trapp family, famously depicted in the 1965 film *The Sound of Music*. These hills are alive!

FASCINATING & TRUE

✓ The von Trapp family escaped Austria in 1938 as it was being taken over by German Nazis just before WWII broke out in 1939. In the 1940s, while on a U.S. tour, the von Trapp family fell in love with the scenery of Stowe, as it reminded them of their Austrian homeland.

✓ There is a family cemetery next to the lodge, where Maria von Trapp and the Baron, also known as "The Captain," are buried. Their children, as well as other members of the family, rest nearby.

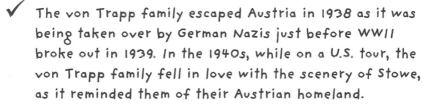

I've been practicing my yodeling for this place!

Enjoy hiking, biking, skiing, swimming, and playing tennis on a real clay court! You're surrounded by 2,500 acres to explore year round. You just pick the season.

Of course, the lodge hosts music classes. Let's get started— "Doe, a deer, a female deer. . . ." You've got the rest!

We love that there's a Mountain Kids Club and Activity Center! No matter what the season, the von Trapps will have the perfect activity to inspire and entertain.

Learn more about this fascinating family and read Maria von Trapp's book, *The Story of the Trapp Family Singers*.

Uh . . . can you save it for the Alps?

BEN & JERRY'S ICE CREAM

1281 WATERBURY-STOWE ROAD, WATERBURY

Middle-school friends and business partners Ben Cohen and Jerry Greenfield started off with an ice cream maker, a $5 ice cream—making class, a renovated gas station, and a whole lot of determination. It *churns* out they were pretty good at it, ultimately selling more than $800-million worth of ice cream every year.

✓ Ben and Jerry are legendary! Their wacky creamery has been concocting ice cream flavors since its opening on May 5, 1978, when they also served soup and crepes!

✓ They have supercool Flavor Gurus who create those unique flavors that our mouths and tummies crave. Need taste testers?

✓ The founders came up with Free Cone Day to celebrate the first year of being open! Today they dish out 1 million free scoops! Thank you!

Ben & Jerry's factory is Vermont's largest attraction. Take a tour and see how they churn out 35,000 pints a day! We like to think it's the Willy Wonka factory of Vermont.

Try one of the more than 30 flavors of Ben & Jerry's ice cream!! Get a double—no, triple—scoop!

Look out for Ben & Jerry's mascot, Woody Jackson the cow. She can be found everywhere! How do we know Woody is a female? She makes milk, silly! Udderly ridiculous!

Visit the Flavor Graveyard with tombstones and creative memorials to 300 flavors. No need to shed any tears at this site unless you're craving "Fossil Fuel," "Peanut Butter and Jelly," or "Dastardly Mash." Who knows! Maybe they'll bring some back from the dead.

Say, "Phish-food!"

Yum! Yum!

CONNECTICUT

Explore 17th-century seaside villages, historic ships, and nuclear-powered submersibles. Celebrate the wonders of aviation and dive into the mysteries of the ocean. Connecticut is the fifth state to join the Union, proudly nicknamed the "Constitution State," "Provisions State," and "Land of Steady Habits." You can guess we'll dig into some serious history here.

MYSTIC

Mystic is a 17th-century seaport village at the mouth of the Mystic River. Home to historic sailing vessels, a maritime museum, and for those who love what's under the sea, an aquarium to boot! Did we mention there's pizza, too?

✓ Mystic's name originates from the Pequot term "missi-tuk," which means "Great Tidal River." The Pequots are Native Americans who live in Connecticut. Since the river meets the ocean by tides and winds, we totally get it!

✓ The Mystic Seaport Museum is the largest maritime museum in the United States. It's home to 500 historic vessels. AHOY, MATE!

✓ The last wooden whaleship in the world is docked here! The *Charles W. Morgan* was called a "lucky ship" because of its many dangerous adventures at sea. It was launched in 1841 to hunt and process whales . . . not so lucky for them.

✓ The main attraction at the Mystic Aquarium are the beluga whales. They are endangered, so this is a unique and special experience.

THINGS TO SEE & DO

☐ Visit the Mystic Seaport Museum and walk through this early-19th-century maritime village.

. . . .

☐ Check out the Discovery Barn's "Force in Motion at Sea" exhibit. This interactive museum includes simple pulley systems, model sailboats, and signal flags . . . plus much more!

. . . .

☐ Tour the *Charles W. Morgan* at Chubb's Wharf. You'll quickly understand why the ship is a National Historic Landmark while gaining an appreciation for why whaling was so important . . . and dangerous.

. . . .

☐ Visit the Mystic Aquarium and say hello to the "canary of the sea," the beluga whale, and the resident penguins.

. . . .

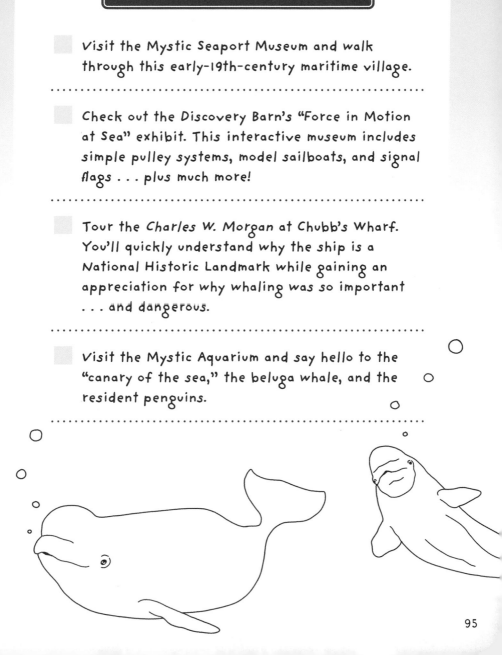

Experience what life was like aboard the once-super-top-secret—and first-ever—nuclear-powered submarine, the USS *Nautilus*. You won't need to go undercover to board this vessel! Call this sub declassified!

EAE
571

I hope this sub sells sandwiches!

FASCINATING & TRUE

✓ On January 21, 1954, twenty thousand people watched the submarine launch into the sea. Her first commanding officer said it best: "Underway on nuclear power."

....

✓ The confident *Nautilus* and her crew became the first to travel under the North Pole in 1958. That's true NORTH!

....

✓ The nuclear reactor of the *Nautilus* operated for two years without refueling. No wonder she was so stealthy! She could reach speeds of 25 miles per hour and dive to 700 feet, staying under for two weeks, because she recycled air and water. (Hope she handled farts, too!). Talk about holding your breath!

....

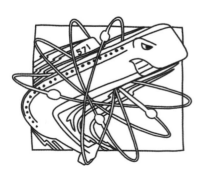

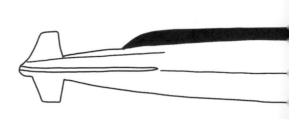

THINGS TO SEE & DO

☐ Board the USS *Nautilus* and imagine what it would be like to be enclosed in this vessel for two weeks straight. Do you think you could do it?

....

☐ Dive into some serious exploration. Take part in the self-guided tours, but don't dive-ulge the secrets of the scavenger hunt!

....

☐ Enjoy a forty-five minute film at the Museum Theater that covers the history of the Submarine Force up through WWII.

....

☐ Ask the staff what it's like to live aboard a sub. Some have even served aboard the *Nautilus* herself. You can bet they have some deep-diving adventure stories for you!

....

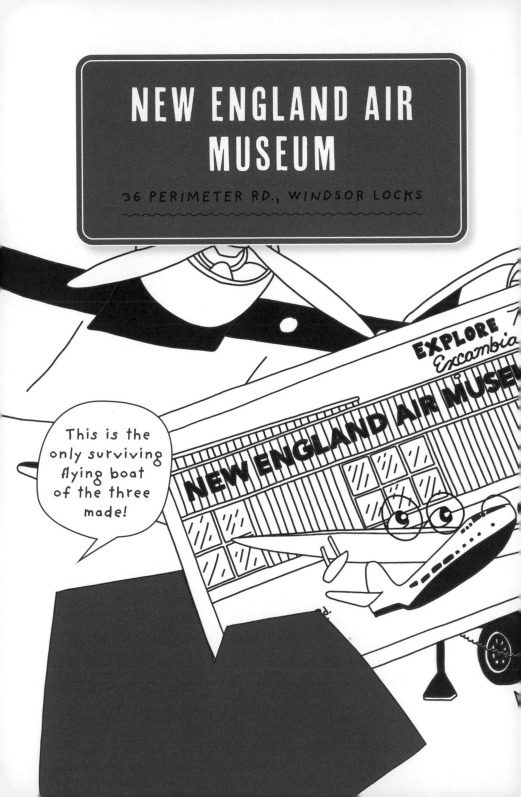

For the aviation buff, this is one spot you won't want to miss. Learn the history of flight by exploring historic and modern aircraft. You'll understand why this is one of the top restoration programs in the country, having preserved many masterpieces of the air for all of us to enjoy!

EXCAMBIAN

I wonder if we can waterski behind it?

FASCINATING & TRUE

✔ There is an outside display and three hangars that house more than 80 historic aircraft. Examine gliders, blimps, even a spacesuit, plus much more! FYI, it's the largest aerospace museum in New England.

....

✔ They have an aviation library, the John W. Ramsay Research Library, and it includes historical photos, blueprints, artwork, and more than 6,000 books. Sorry, no checking out these materials. You'll have to look through them while you're there.

....

✔ The French Blériot XI on exhibit was built in 1909 and was the very first commercially built aircraft. It may not look like much, but it started the foundation for the aircraft manufacturing industry.

....

✔ Don't miss the flying boat Excambian and her 124-foot wingspan (that's more than three school buses in length)! Just one of three aircraft that were built, she is the only one still around.

....

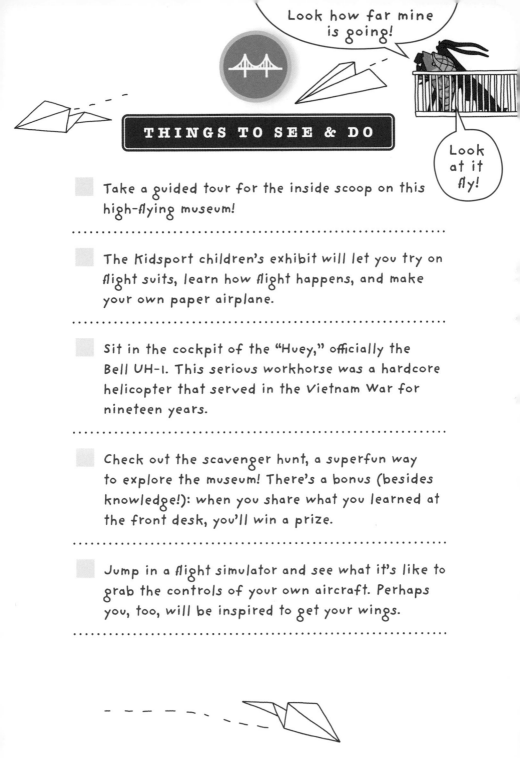

Look how far mine is going!

Look at it fly!

THINGS TO SEE & DO

Take a guided tour for the inside scoop on this high-flying museum!

....

The Kidsport children's exhibit will let you try on flight suits, learn how flight happens, and make your own paper airplane.

....

Sit in the cockpit of the "Huey," officially the Bell UH-1. This serious workhorse was a hardcore helicopter that served in the Vietnam War for nineteen years.

....

Check out the scavenger hunt, a superfun way to explore the museum! There's a bonus (besides knowledge!): when you share what you learned at the front desk, you'll win a prize.

....

Jump in a flight simulator and see what it's like to grab the controls of your own aircraft. Perhaps you, too, will be inspired to get your wings.

....

RHODE ISLAND

Welcome to the smallest state in the U.S. Rhode Island is famous for yachtsmen, Gilded Age mansions, sandy beaches, and the ever-so-popular "stuffies." Put on your Bluchers, pack a picnic, and set your sails into the wind—this is Rhode Island.

NEWPORT

The city of Newport is located on Aquidneck Island along Narragansett Bay. It has been the summer residence of some of the country's wealthiest families. With cliffside walks and endless ocean views, no wonder it's a top destination. So turn up your collar, put on your Bermuda shorts, and let's get exploring!

FASCINATING & TRUE

✔ Sailing the waters off Newport has attracted superskilled yachtsmen from around the world. It even held the America's Cup trophy, the "Auld Mug," from 1851 to 1957. That's 132 years!

. . . .

✔ Every year, 250,000 people hike along the Cliff Walk, a coastal path with beautiful views of the ocean. Along the way, you'll be able to access the century-old Gilded Age estates. Be careful, there are large rocks to pass, poison ivy, and supersteep drops. Keep those feet steady!

. . . .

✔ The Newport Tower in Touro Park has been a tourist attraction since the 1800s! Mainly because nobody knows how it got there. They say Vikings built it in 1150 or perhaps the Knights Templar in 1398. It even aligns with the stars as a way to tell time. Bottom line: it's a mystery!

. . . .

THINGS TO SEE & DO

Visit Easton's Beach, also called First Beach. Build a sandcastle, take a swim, then swing by the Save the Bay Exploration Center and Aquarium. With three touch tanks and a knowledgeable staff, you'll leave knowing lots about local sea creatures and how to protect them. Our favorite cause!

....

Take on the Cliff Walk. The 3.5-mile-long trail passes through a National Historic District as it winds through 100-year-old mega-mansions of the 19th century.

....

Explore the Breakers, the famous summer residence of the wealthy Vanderbilt family, with an audio tour. Be sure to look out for the lions, dolphins, and dragons! They're all Vander-built!

What's up with this super-fancy pitcher?

AMERICAS CUP

It's not a pitcher, Shrimp. It's the prized Auld Mug!

NARRAGANSETT

✓ The town's name comes from the Narragansett Native Americans who were local to the region. "Narragansett" means "people of the small point" in their native language. In 1658 and 1659, the land was purchased by English settlers who really got "the point."

✓ The Narragansett Pier Casino was built in the 1880s. It became one of America's most prominent resorts and is famous for its iconic granite towers.

✓ Hey! Our favorite green thumb, Frederick Law Olmsted, designed the landscape for the Towers! He is famous for designing many other favorite city escapes, including New York City's Central Park, Chicago's Jackson Park, and Boston's Emerald Necklace.

Welcome to one of New England's top beach towns. Cruise the boardwalk, dine on locally caught seafood, and relax on a beach that has made this seaside town a top destination for ocean lovers for more than 100 years!

THINGS TO SEE & DO

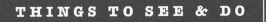 Walk under the archway of the Towers, the iconic symbol of Gansett!

....

Visit the late 1800s Coast Guard House. Originally a Coast Guard station perched above Narragansett Bay, it was turned into a restaurant in the 1940s. Today, it serves (GULP!) locally caught seafood. We are definitely not locals here!

....

Dig up some quahogs (pronounced "co-hog"). New Englanders love these clams! Then try some stuffies—a local way of saying "stuffed clams." Eat enough and you'll be stuffed, too.

....

Holy mackerel, what a trip! What did you think about our adventure throughout New England? Did anything stand out to you? Were you a nature buff? Or perhaps you preferred the history and city exploration? If you're not quite sure, just keep this adventure book handy and revisit these awesome places in your own time. But if you're ready to plan your expedition, write down your favorite places as a shortcut. Plotting your course (just like a sea captain) makes it an easy way to know where you're going!

LIST THE PLACES YOU'D LIKE TO SEE IN NEW ENGLAND:

1

2

3

4

5

HERE ARE A FEW SUGGESTIONS!

We loved hiking up Maine's Cadillac Mountain to watch the first sunrise on the continent. And mugging for the camera at Rockefeller's Teeth.

Exploring Massachusetts, the WHOI center, and the Titanic exhibit was claw-pinching. And enjoying ice cream at Vermont's Ben & Jerry's was a sweet treat. Finally, taking in the historic town of Boston—we mean Beantown—was especially fun. Okay, we get it, it's a lot. I think we're going to go through this book a few times, too!

The best thing about this trip is exploring all these sites with you. You have also become wicked-smaht about New England! Ayuh? Ayuh! Have you noticed how connected we are to our neighbors across the pond? (That's the Atlantic Ocean!) Ei-fel, that is, WE feel another great adventure is just over the horizon!

Your salty bffs,

Shrimp 'n Lobster

Thank you!

Come again!

ACKNOWLEDGMENTS

This series would not be possible without the support and guidance of Angela Engel and her rock stars at the Collective Book Studio, pun master and mentor Jeff Myers, my dear friend Sharon Fox, and most importantly my parents who set me on the path to get out there and see the world. Mah, this journey is for you.

ABOUT THE AUTHOR

Charlotte Rygh's passion for exploring the oceans provides inspiration for her unique illustrations. She is a graduate of the Kanbar Institute of Film and Television at NYU's Tisch School of the Arts, and she currently calls the San Francisco Bay Area her home. To Learn more about Charlotte's work, and her two favorite crustaceans, visit shrimpnlobster.com.